OCTOBER 12-2000

DEAR Robbie:

I hope to be able to take you to
Mont St Michel when you are
a little older.

love,

grand'Mère

Catalogue
A catalogue of our editions is available on request from,
MSM B.P. 20 65502 Vic-en-Bigorre Cedex (France)
Tel.: (33) 05 62 31 68 01, Fax.: (33) 05 62 31 68 08
http://www.msm-editions.fr
e-mail: contact@msm-editions.fr

© **MSM**, 1996

BP 20, 65500 Vic-en-Bigorre - France

Dépôt légal: March 2000
ISBN: 2-909998-05-3
Printed in Belgium by Casterman SA, Tournai

Jeremy

A child at Mont-Saint-Michel

Illustrations : Gemma Sales
Written by : Jean Hennegé

Translated by : Louise Leteux

Jeremy and his parents are going to visit his grandmother who lives in Saint Malo. On the way they go to Mont-Saint-Michel to spend the night, something they have always done since Jeremy was a little boy. As the car approaches, the Mount looks just like a giant spinning top which has come to rest on the sand. Swirls of mist cling to the pinnacles and, way up at the top the golden statue of archangel Saint Michel shimmers in the last rays of the setting sun. The car reaches the causeway, in five minutes they will be there.

There are nearly one hundred steps up to the hotel. Here, wherever you go it is either up or down, up to the sky, or down towards the sea. On the horizon, Mount Dol and Mount Tombelaine rise out of the sand. It is high tide, soon the base of the Mount will be in the water.

Jeremy has his own room with a big bed all to himself. At the reception desk they had told him that he was a big boy now, ten years old, he no longer needs to share his parents bedroom. On the walls of his room there are fourteen engravings recounting the history of the Mount. Jeremy looks at them. His father would say that he should study them but he is on holiday. Jeremy falls asleep and dreams.

Here is Saint Michel, the archangel. He symbolises the fight between good and evil. Saint Michel slayed a nine-headed dragon who was terrorising the area and making the stars fall out of the sky. The legend tells of how the battle was fought above the Mount, which long ago was called Mount Tombe. It is this story and many others which made the Mount so famous and gave it its present name: Mont-Saint-Michel.

A legend from the Middle Ages recounts the origin of the Mount. Archangel Saint Michel, the slayer of dragons asked Bishop Aubert of Avranches to build a place of prayer on earth, here on Mount Tombe. One night in the year 708 a bull came to the Mount, nobody knows how and traced a large circle on the grass. The legend also tells how Bishop Aubert made fresh water pour from a rock by striking it with his cross, thus enabling people to live on the mount.

The recorded history of the Mount starts in the eighth century with the nomination of twelve canons installed on a huge deserted rock in the middle of the sea, which was to become, two centuries later, Mont-Saint-Michel. In 911, the Vikings aboard their powerful longboats attacked and conquered all the towns within their reach, all, except Mont-Saint-Michel. From this period dates the Carolingian church, today known as Notre-Dame-Sous-Terre.

At sunrise the Benedictine monks living here since 966 go to the new Romanesque church to sing their songs. The monks entire life is devoted to work, reading the sacred texts and prayer. They live their lives as Saint Benoit said they should, they have a code of behaviour, rules they must follow day in, day out for the rest of their lives.

Alas! Mont-Saint-Michel "in peril of the sea" is also Mont-Saint-Michel in peril of fire! In 1112 a huge fire is started by lightning. The walls of the abbey give way and the flames reach the other buildings within. Everything has to be rebuilt. Throughout the history of the Mount there will be many more fires and much rebuilding will have to be done.

Raoul of the Islands will make of Mont-Saint-Michel an example for all future builders. It will be so magnificient that travellers will wonder at its beauty, calling it "the marvel". Right at the bottom there will be a huge room to welcome the poor people and the travellers. Right at the top will be the monks domain, the last rays of the setting sun lighting up this level. In the middle is the host-hall, here the visiting kings are received. Building starts in 1210 and lasts eighteen years, a short time for the period.

In the scriptorium the monks recopy and decorate the manuscripts. Here in the twelfth century, books are entirely hand made. Much is written at Mont-Saint-Michel and illuminated. This is the way the monks decorate the written manuscripts by painting over the black ink in gold and beautiful colours. A reed pen is used to write, made out of a piece of reed sharpened to a fine point enabling the complicated letters to be formed. The monks write on tanned lamb hide called parchment as there is no paper.

The Hundred Years war! Soldiers, robbers and the plague are everywhere. Archangel Saint Michel appears before a young shepherdess called Joan of Arc. From the island of Tombelaine the English attack Mont-Saint-Michel. With culverins and many other types of cannon of the era, they bombard the Mount with a hail of fire and iron. All in vain! The Mount will never surrender!

The English boats sail with the tides, night and day, stopping all supplies reaching the Mount. In a final attack, the town, entirely built out of timber is destroyed. Once again the abbey walls crumble. Everything must be rebuilt, but the Mount will never surrender!

There have always been pilgrimages to the Mount. Kings as well as children come from far and wide to pray to Saint Michel and to seek pardon for their sins. A crowd of children wait for low tide to cross the sands on foot, which separate the Mount from the main land. After which there is the slow and difficult climb up towards the summit.

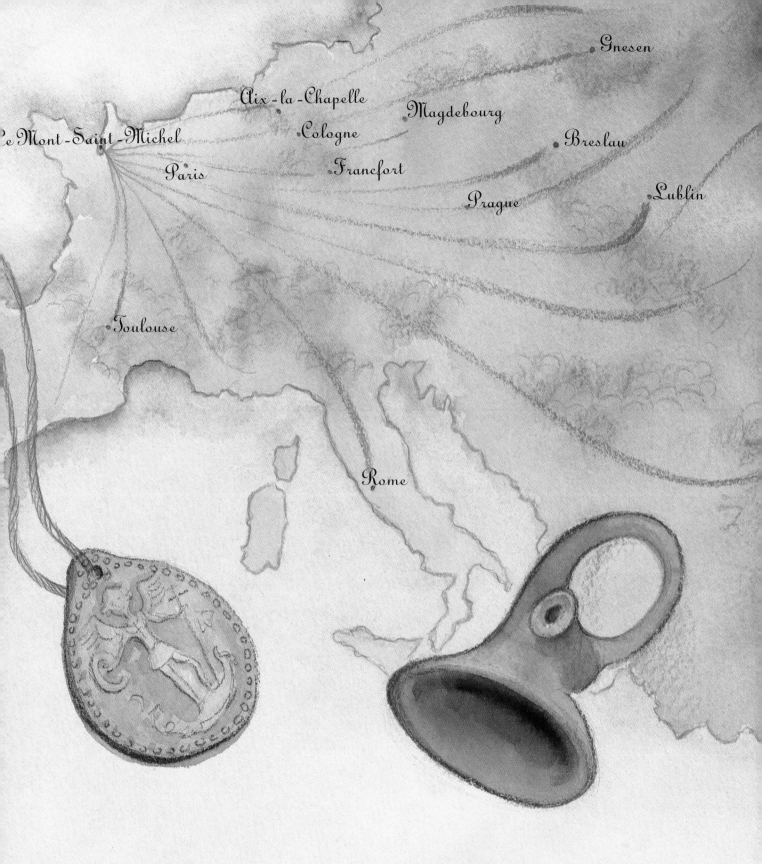

Gnesen

Aix-la-Chapelle

Magdebourg

e Mont-Saint-Michel

Cologne

Breslau

Paris

Francfort

Prague

Lublin

Toulouse

Rome

This final climb is nothing compared to the hundreds of miles these young pilgrims have already travelled. Many of whom come from Poland, Germany and Switzerland. They have left their families, homes and villages, to come to the Mount. They are the shepherds, boys and girls, the young guardians of the flocks. They will return home with emblems and medallions, souvenirs of Saint Michel.

The religious wars of the sixteenth century ravaged France dividing it into two camps: protestants and catholics. The Mount is fortified to weather this new storm. Behind the thick ramparts the Mount's inhabitants watch as the sea rises towards the enemy troops. It comes as quickly as a galloping horse! Nine times the fort is attacked and nine times the town resists. The Mount is impregnable!

In 1662 there are only sixteen old and poor monks left on the Mount. The past splendours and all the famous legends are dead and forgotten. People no longer believe in archangel Saint Michel, the Mount no longer serves a purpose.

During the French Revolution the Mount becomes a prison. There will be as many as seven hundred and fifty prisoners, men and women in the "Bastille in the sea", ironically known as Mount Freedom. The Mount will serve as a prison for almost a century. When the prisoners are not underground in their cells, they work in the workshops installed throughout the abbey.

In the nineteenth century the Mount finally sinks into oblivion. The granite giant forgotten by time, slumbers, its head in the grey clouds and its feet in the sea. Famous visitors such as Victor Hugo come to visit, paying homage to its glorious past. One fine day the decision is taken to wake up the stone giant and an architect called Corroyer is appointed. He takes on the task of rebuilding the Mount stone by stone.

A causeway is built allowing passage to the Mount at high and at low tide. A small steam engine runs along the causeway to the city walls. Way up at the top of the abbey, on the point of the wrought iron steeple, a statue of archangel Saint Michel is erected, made of copper covered with gold leaf.

The Mount has no protection from the passing years, nor from man. The sea which once protected it barely reaches the city walls now. Mont-Saint-Michel is gradually silting-up. There are three rivers flowing into the bay bringing with them thousands of tons of sand. If we are not very careful, perhaps one day the landscape will look as it did in Jeremy's nightmare.

It is eight o'clock in the morning. The early morning sunlight streams through Jeremy's curtains. What a strange dream! A dream as long as a history lesson. It is time to get up. Grandmother is waiting for us.

Nowadays Mont-Saint-Michel welcomes millions of visitors every year. Tourists come from all over the world to visit one of the most beautiful sites in France. Jeremy has left with his parents. But they will be back next year; that is a promise.